Printed in France by Amazon
Brétigny-sur-Orge, FR

16590184R00069